# The
# Friendly
# Beasts

## A Medieval French Carol

Adapted and illustrated by
### Jan Burlingham

Ambassador
Children's Books
New York/Mahwah, NJ

Library of Congress Cataloging-in-Publication Data

Burlingham, Jan.
  The friendly beasts : a medieval French carol / adapted and illustrated by Jan Burlingham.
      p. cm.
  Summary: In this traditional English Christmas carol based on a medieval French song, the stable beasts tell of the gifts they have given to the newborn Jesus.
  ISBN 978-0-8091-6742-5 (alk. paper)
  1.  Carols, English--England--Texts. 2.  Christmas music--Texts. 3. Folk songs, English--England--Texts. [1. Carols, English. 2. Christmas music. 3. Folk songs, English.] I. Title.
  PZ8.3.B95265Fr 2009
  782.28'1723--dc22
  [E]
                                    2009006427

Published by Ambassador Books
An imprint of Paulist Press
997 Macarthur Boulevard
Mahwah, NJ 07430

www.ambassadorbooks.com

Printed and bound in China.

# To Benjamin

"Beasts be with you."
"And also with you…"

Was humbly born
in a stable rude,

And the friendly beasts
around Him stood,

Jesus our brother,
kind and good.

"I," said the donkey,
all shaggy and brown,
"I carried His mother
up hill and down;

"I carried her safely
to Bethlehem town."
"I," said the donkey, all
shaggy and brown.

"I," said the cow
all white and red,
"I gave Him my manger
for His bed;
I gave Him my hay
to pillow His head."
"I," said the cow
all white and red.

"I," said the sheep
with curly horn,
"I gave Him my wool
for a blanket warm;

"He wore my coat
on Christmas morn."
"I," said the sheep
with curly horn.

"I," said the dove
from the rafters high,
"I cooed Him to sleep
so He would not cry;

"We cooed Him to sleep,
my mate and I."
"I," said the dove
from the rafters high.

Thus every beast
by some good spell,
in the stable dark
was glad to tell

# Of the gift he gave Emmanuel.

# The Friendly Beasts

## A Note on the Carol

This carol traces its roots to the 12th century Latin hymn *Orientis Partibus*. The hymn was sung as part of a church ceremony celebrating the flight of the Holy Family to Egypt. The Donkey's Festival (Fête de l'Âne) was a mass that included leading a donkey into the church sometimes ridden by the town's prettiest maiden. These celebrations were documented circa 1222 in Sens, France.